CANADIAN ROCKIES
PANORAMA

Stephen Flagler

ALTITUDE PUBLISHING
Canadian Rockies/Vancouver

Waterton and the Prince of Wales Hotel, Waterton Lakes National Park

OVERLEAF: Sunrise on Lake Louise, Banff National Park

OPPOSITE: Mule Deer on the shores of Waterton Lakes, Waterton Lakes National Park

Red Rock Canyon, Waterton Lakes National Park

The Three Sisters and the Bow River, Kananaskis Country

King Canyon, Kananaskis Country

OPPOSITE: Beaver Dam in front of Mt. Kidd, Kananaskis Country

Sunrise on Mt. Assiniboine, Mt. Assiniboine Provincial Park

OPPOSITE: Mt. Assiniboine and the Lodge, Mt. Assiniboine Provincial Park

Bow Falls and Cascade Mountain, Banff National Park

OVERLEAF: Mt. Assiniboine and surrounding peaks, Mt. Assiniboine National Park

The Bow River with the Fairholme Range in the background, Banff National Park

The Banff Springs Golf Course with Tunnel and Cascade Mountains, Banff National Park

OPPOSITE: The Banff Springs Hotel, Banff National Park

Cascade Mountain and the Bow River, Banff National Park

OPPOSITE: Cascade Mountain and Banff Avenue, Banff National Park

Mt. Rundle and the Vermilion Lakes in winter, Banff National Park

OPPOSITE: Mt. Rundle and the first Vermilion Lake, Banff National Park

The Hoodoos with the Banff Springs Hotel in the background, Banff National Park

Lake Minnewanka, Banff National Park

The Lower Falls in Johnston Canyon, Banff National Park

OPPOSITE: Castle Mountain, Banff National Park

Mountain stream in the Canadian Rockies

OPPOSITE: Mt. Bident and the Tower of Babel near Moraine Lake, Banff National Park

Consolation Lake near Moraine Lake, Banff National Park

OPPOSITE: Reflections in Moraine Lake, Banff National Park

Mt. Temple from Saddle Mountain, Lake Louise, Banff National Park

OPPOSITE: Lake Louise, Banff National Park

Lake Louise and the Chateau from the air, Banff National Park

OPPOSITE: Flower beds at Chateau Lake Louise, Banff National Park

Chateau Lake Louise, Banff National Park

OVERLEAF: Mt. Lefroy and Mt. Victoria at Lake Louise, Banff National Park

OPPOSITE: Lake O'Hara, Yoho National Park

Mt. Hungabee and Lake Lefroy, Yoho National Park

OPPOSITE: Autumn Larches on Opabin Plateau, near Lake O'Hara, Yoho National Park

The Natural Bridge over the Kicking Horse River, Yoho National Park

OPPOSITE: Rainbow over Cathedral Mountain, Yoho National Park

Takakkaw Falls, Yoho National Park

Emerald Lake, Yoho National Park

Lake Louise Mountains reflected in Herbert Lake, Banff National Park

OPPOSITE: Crowfoot Glacier on the Icefields Parkway, Banff National Park

Bow Lake, Banff National Park

OPPOSITE: Peyto Lake and the Mistaya Valley, Banff National Park

Sunset on Mt. Wilson, Banff National Park

OPPOSITE: Freshfield Icefield near Saskatchewan Crossing, Banff National Park

Athabasca Glacier, Jasper National Park

OPPOSITE: Snowmobiles on Athabasca Glacier, Jasper National Park

Mt. Kerkeslin and Horseshoe Lake, Jasper National Park

OVERLEAF: Mt. Athabasca, Mt. Andromeda and the Athabasca Glacier, Jasper National Park

OPPOSITE: Sunwapta Falls, Jasper National Park

Angel Glacier on Mt. Edith Cavell, Jasper National Park

OPPOSITE: Mount Edith Cavell and Cavell Lake, Jasper National Park

The Jasper Tramway with the town of Jasper below, Jasper National Park

OPPOSITE: Lac Beauvert at Jasper Park Lodge, Jasper National Park

Sunset on Medicine Lake, Jasper National Park

OPPOSITE: Pyramid Mountain and Pyramid Lake, Jasper National Park

Maligne Lake, Jasper National Park

OPPOSITE: Spirit Island on Maligne Lake, Jasper National Park

Maligne Canyon, Jasper National Park

OPPOSITE: Mt. Robson and the Robson River, Jasper National Park

Copyright © 1993/1996/1999
Altitude Publishing Canada Ltd.
The Canadian Rockies
1500 Railway Avenue
Canmore, Alberta
Canada T1W 1P6
ISBN 1-55153-100-3
9 8 7 6 5 4

Text and photo selection: Stephen Flagler
Editor: Elizabeth Wilson
Design: Robert MacDonald, MediaClones Inc.

Made in Western Canada
Printed and bound in Western Canada by Friesen Printers, Altona Manitoba

Altitude GreenTree Program
Altitude will plant in Western Canada twice as many trees as were used in the manufacturing of this book.

Mt. Robson from Berg Lake, Jasper National Park

FRONT COVER PHOTO: Moraine Lake in the Valley of the Ten Peaks
BACK COVER PHOTOS: Maligne Lake (top), and Indian Paintbrush (bottom)
INSIDE COVER PHOTOS: Byron Harmon photos courtesy of the Whyte Museum of the Canadian Rockies: Mt. Robson, 1913 (inside front), and Mt. Quincy, 1924 (inside back)

Photo Credits: Van Christou: 4; Don Harmon: front cover, 1, 5, 6, 8, 9, 10/11, 12, 13, 16, 17, 19, 26, 27, 28, 29, 31, 35, 37, 40, 41, 43, 44, 45, 48, 50/51, 52, 55, 57, 62, 63, back cover top; Carole Harmon: 14, 15, 18, 21, 23, 32/33, 34, 42, 54, 58, 60, 61, 64; Stephen Hutchings: 7, 20, 22, 24, 25, 36, 38, 39, 47, 53, 56, 59, back cover bottom; Scott Rowed: 2, 3, 30, 46; R. W. Sandford: 49